NANNA NOMORE

Kelly Anne Barnacle

NANNA NOMORE

© 2023 Kelly Anne Barnacle

All rights reserved.

Presentation by *BookLeaf Publishing*

Web: www.bookleafpub.com

E-mail: info@bookleafpub.com

ISBN: 9789357748476

First edition 2023

*To our darling Baby Grandson Ronnie Joe -
Loved Always*

PREFACE

Ronnie Joe, Nanna loves you very much, wish I were writing you birthday cards instead.

Nanna Nomore

I'd assumed tomorrow was a given
in the summer sales I brought him fox woollen
mittens.
his cold now they will never cure,
I am his Nanna Nomore.

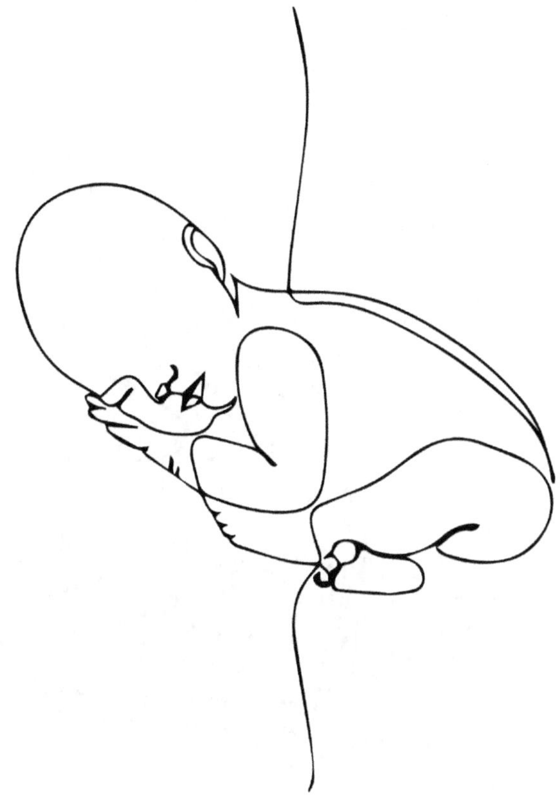

Songs I can no longer listen to

I'd write the list,
but it's vast and long
I wouldn't want to miss
a single shitty song,
I can no longer listen to
now you are gone.

1992

1992
not the year
a count
an account
his hours
time now after is now numerous, forever plenty
e   n   d   l   e   s   s
so far it's two thousand nine hundred and twenty

Forever Young

Forever young
Forever gone.
His few firsts became his lasts,
his only one.

Endless

5

Grief and guilt merged
that August summer night.
We're relentlessly
mourning that marriage,
no divorce or separation in sight.

Hope

Do you have hope some I could borrow,
to paste together my tomorrow?
Could you spare a slice,
just a drip, tears of mice?
I don't want to ask, to beg, to plead
but they said I must have it,
it's what my life needs.

Seeds of Hope

seeds planted
for first taste veg
rot in their grave graves
disposal I dread

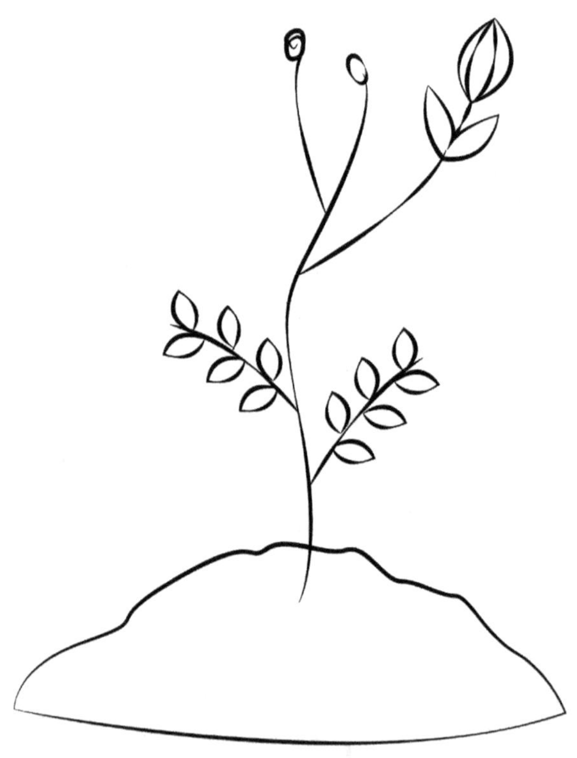

Learning Lines

I practiced, He Died, in my head, in my heart, internally over and over, in prep for the questions, but nothing prepares for the actual sound of the words coming out of me. Echoing. He passed away didn't impact. We lost him was too careless, he wasn't parked up his pram and forgotten about. Gone to heaven, where, you sure, can I write or call? Passed over, we didn't exchange him, handed him off like a charity donation, pass the parcel, someone else's turn now, his time with us was complete, but the music still plays and she sits empty-handed.

The Scream

There is nothing,
absolute nothing,
zero,
nowt,
nought that compares,
to the sound of a grieving mother.
I could write a million words on this but I'll not
write another.

Top ten list of things people say that help after the sudden and unexpected death of a baby

1.

2.

3.

4.

5.

6.

7.

8.

9.

10.

Me Me Me

This
These letters
These words
A selfish self-centred creation
It's not about me but them, her
& my own first-born son

GRAVEYARD SHIFT

Grieving grave gardeners,
tears sobbingly watering everything.
Tiny dreadful deadful allotments, cultivated by
seaside windmills, tethered balloons, damp
bears,
constantly constructing fairy-sized fairgrounds.
Some eventually just let mother nature persist.
No gossip over fences.
No lawn envy.
No baby grave maintenance Olympics.

Something at Least

I'm glad my dad is sometimes away with the
fairies,
so I've never lied.
He doesn't always remember his great-grandson
being born,
so I need not remind him he died.

Unearned Title

I am still a Nanna
Just his Nanna?
No small handprints on the fridge
No tiny wellies in the boot

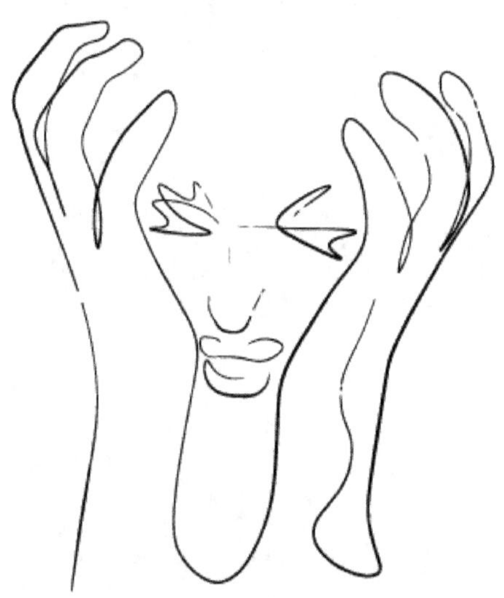

Old Story

There is a children's story I remember. The sly fox sneaks into Goats' house when she has popped to the market. Fox then eats the little goat's kids. The Goat, mortified of course, tracks him down, waits until he sleeps the deep sleep of a sly fox that has just had a goat kid all you can eat buffet, Goat then pulls out her long sharp dressmaking scissors and cuts him open. Goat pulls out the baby kids, all amazingly alive and very delighted to see her. Then they fill him back up with rocks and stitch him together with crude big black stitches.

New Story

I felt joy, calm, peace and even hope, all shiny little marbles rolling around inside. Totally unsure if they were really mine, had I siphoned them, stolen them, snitched them away from some other searching soul?
Then I slept, awaking with a telephone call, it was like Goat had come slit me open, to take back what was not ever really mine, filling me with the rocks of despair, grief and guilt. Heavy. Ancient. Stitched me back up and I try breathing now with the weight.

Packing

try again
pick up
smell
hug
smell
put down
pick up
hug
fold
smell
unfold
smell
hug
fold
pack
unpack
unfold
hug
smell
fold
unfold
put down
hug
fold
put away
close drawer
turn off the light
gently pull the door to
next time

Grandma Grief

Grandma Grief moved in,
apparently she is staying a while,
dragged all she had like a near-dead dog,
whimpering.
She sits, rocking all hours, in my chair.
(Action here - breathe in nice and steady, hold 3
seconds breathe out, now ready for the last line)
We welcome her now, the reflection of our love,
huge & constant.

Sharing...

I don't want to tell it
You don't want to hear it
but the writing of it lets it out
still a beast
still a burden
just at least
a more empty dungeon

meet me in my dreams

we'd sit on the swing
I'd read him all the books
listening to old records
it would be the golden hour
warm skin and freckles

Sanctuary

Memory, its a stick
to beat or steady myself
or its a rope
to hang or tether myself
or maybe a room
where I shut the door, hanker down or
where I sit and send invites out